A Let's-Read-and-Find-Out Book™

REVISED EDITION

SNOW IS FALLING

by Franklyn M. Branley · illustrated by Holly Keller

A Harper Trophy Book
Harper & Row, Publishers

The *Let's-Read-and-Find-Out Book*™ series was originated by Dr. Franklyn M. Branley, Astronomer Emeritus and former Chairman of the American Museum–Hayden Planetarium, and was formerly co-edited by him and Dr. Roma Gans, Professor Emeritus of Childhood Education, Teachers College, Columbia University. Text and illustrations are checked for accuracy by an expert in the relevant field.

Library of Congress Cataloging-in-Publication Data

Branley, Franklyn Mansfield, 1915—
  Snow is falling.

  (Let's-read-and-find-out science book)
  Summary: Describes the characteristics of snow,
its usefulness to plants and animals, and the hazards
it can cause.
  1. Snow—Juvenile literature. [1. Snow] I. Keller,
Holly, ill. II. Title III. Series
QC929.S7B7 1986   551.57'84   85-48256
ISBN 0-690-04547-6
ISBN 0-690-04548-4 (lib. bdg.)
ISBN 0-06-445058-9 (pbk.)

SNOW IS FALLING

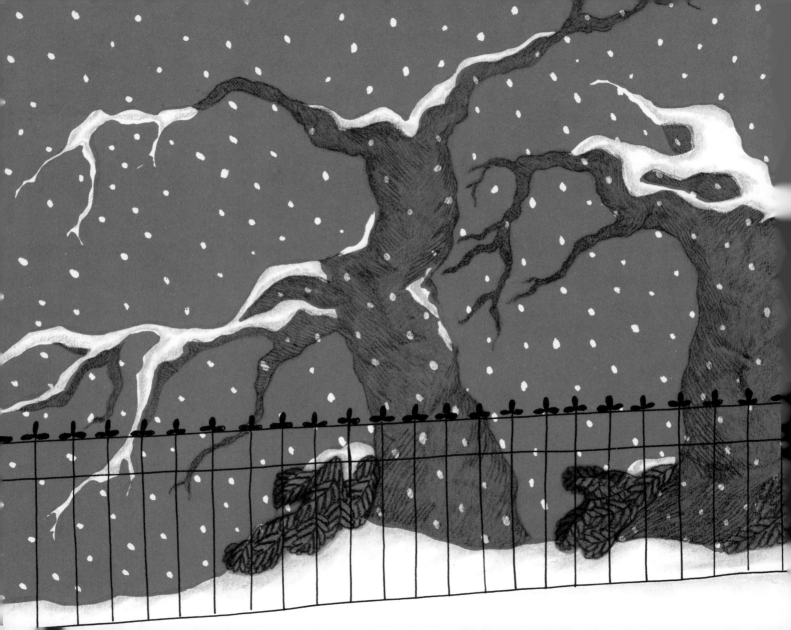

Night has come and snow is falling. It falls without a sound. Look at the streetlight. You can see snow falling in front of it. The snow may fall all night.

The snow may fall all day. The snow gets deeper and deeper. The lawn is white. The trees are white, and so are the roofs of houses. Everything is covered. Everything is white. Everything is quiet and cold.

It is always cold when snow falls. It is so cold that water vapor freezes in the air. This makes snowflakes. Let a snowflake fall on your mitten. The snowflake may be big. It may be small.

If the snowflake is very small, look at it through a magnifying glass. A magnifying glass makes things look bigger. Count the sides on each snowflake. Each snowflake has six sides. Each snowflake is different, but each one has six sides.

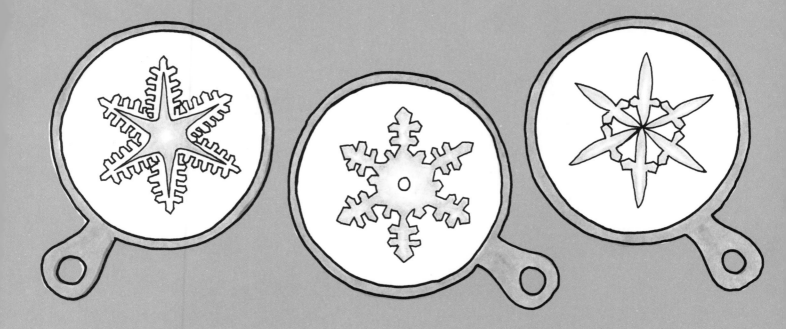

The snowflake will look like this,   or this,   or like this.

Sometimes snow is wet and sticky. When you walk in wet, sticky snow, you splash, and slip, and slide. Sometimes snow is light, dry, and fluffy. Walking through light snow is fun. You can kick it into the air. You can scoop up a big shovelful of light, dry snow.

You can run and roll and ski in the snow. You can slide on your sled. You can build a snowman.

Snow can be fun, but what does snow do? Is it good for plants? Is it good for animals? Is it good for you and me? Let's find out.

Snow covers plants that must stay in the ground all winter. The snow is like a blanket. Because the plants are covered, wind, ice, and cold cannot hurt them. Plants that are covered with snow can live through the cold winter. Snow is good for plants.

Snow is good for many animals, too. Worms and mice, moles and chipmunks, stay under the ground all winter. The blanket of snow keeps the wind and cold from the animals. Snow helps to keep them warm. You can see how this works.

Get two thermometers. Bury one thermometer in the snow. Hang the other thermometer outdoors. Hang it from a tree or beside a window.

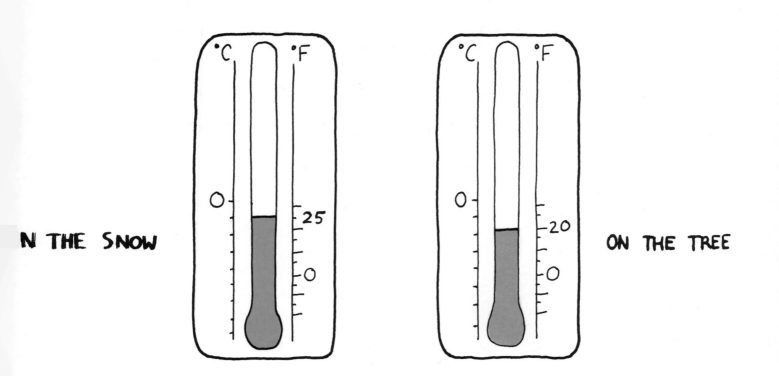

N THE SNOW

ON THE TREE

After an hour, uncover the thermometer in the snow.
What is the temperature? Look at the other thermometer.
What is the temperature? Where is it colder? Snow
protects many plants and animals from the wind and cold.

Snow protects people, too. In the far north, Eskimos sometimes make houses of snow. They cut out blocks from the hard, packed snow. They pile the blocks high to make a snow house. The snow house is called an igloo. Inside the igloo, Eskimos keep snug and warm.

Snow is good in other ways. Melted snow gives us water for our wells, our streams, and our rivers.

When winter is over, the sun warms the snow. The snow melts slowly, and water goes into the soil. The soil becomes crumbly. Plants grow well in the loose, moist, warm soil.

Sometimes snow is not good. When strong winds blow, the soft, quiet snow becomes a howling blizzard. A blizzard makes life hard for animals and people. When snow piles high, it may be so deep that animals cannot move. The snow covers their food. Cars may get stuck. Power lines may blow down.

The deep snows of winter may melt fast in the spring.
There is more water than streams can carry. The streams
overflow. There may be floods.

Snow can make life hard. But it is fun to run, roll, and ski in.

Snow gives us water for wells, streams, and rivers.
Snow is good for plants and animals. Snow is good
for people.

It is good for you and me.